The Uncallused Hand

poems

The Uncallused Hand

poems

WALKER ABEL

HOMEBOUND
PUBLICATIONS
Independent Publisher of Contemplative Titles
STONINGTON, CONNECTICUT

PUBLISHED BY HOMEBOUND PUBLICATIONS

Homebound Publications books may be purchased for educational, business, or sales promotional use. For information please write: Special Markets Department, Homebound Publications, PO Box 1442, Pawcatuck, CT 06379

Visit us www.homeboundpublications.com

FIRST EDITION

ISBN: 978-1-938846-40-3
Book Designed by Leslie M. Browning
Cover Images by © "Rain" by Ivan Yendogurov (Public Domain)

Library of Congress Cataloging-in-Publication Data

Abel, Walker.
    [Poems. Selections]
    The uncallused hand : poems / by Walker Abel. — First edition.
        pages cm
    ISBN 978-1-938846-40-3 (pbk.)
    I. Title.
    PS3601.B436A6 2014
    811'.6--dc23
                                                    2014022243

10 9 8 7 6 5 4 3 2 1

Homebound Publications holds a fervor for environmental conservation. We are ever-mindful of our "carbon footprint". Our books are printed on paper with chain of custody certification from the Forest Stewardship Council, Sustainable Forestry Initiative, and the Programme for the Endorsement of Forest Certification. This ensures that, in every step of the process, from the tree to the reader's hands, that the paper our books are printed on has come from sustainably managed forests. Furthermore, each year Homebound Publications donates 1% of our annual income to an ecological or humanitarian charity. To learn more about this year's charity visit www.homeboundpublications.com.

For Willow

because what rises to the endurance of symbol and myth has origin in the frailty of lived experience.

Contents

Section 1: Thirteen Ways of Seeing You

Scarf   3
Bird   4
Night   5
Door   6
Deer   7
Flower   8
Heron   9
Chickadees   10
Sway   11
Sheen   12
Invitation   13
Closer   14
Swallows   15

Section 2: She Said

Junco   21
Bird Song   22
Moon   23
Beauty Trail   24
Strawberries   26
Deer Beds   28
Mermaid   29
Triumph   30
River   31
Dogwood Bloom   32
Reluctant Farewell at a Small Sierran Lake   34

Section 3: Once Upon a Time

Once	41
Rock, Fence Posts, Snow	43
Almost Home	45
Three Men Pass	46
Wild Iris, Lost Coast	47
Frog by Granite Creek	48
Taste	49
Desert Boat	50
Breaking Camp After Ten Days Under Desert Cottonwoods	51
Sonoran Rhythms	52

Section 4: Zen

Desert Rain	59
Juniper Branch	60
The Mechanic	61
The Way of the Shower	62
After Singing	63
Desert Music	64
I Lean and Loaf in White Mountain Day	65
Wine	66
Four Aces	67
Empty Round Bowl	69
On a Treeless High Mountain Ridge	70
Under a Tree Looking Up	71
Remembering Chuang Tzu in the California Desert	72

Laundry   73
Leaf   74
A Day   75

Epilogue

Uncallused Hand   81

About the Author
About the Press

Thirteen Ways of
Seeing You

As I see my soul reflected in Nature,
As I see through a mist, One with inexpressible completeness, sanity, beauty,
See the bent head and arms folded over the breast, the Female I see.
—WALT WHITMAN

Fairy tales afford a glimpse into the phenomenology of panpsychism, that the quest for love
that is so often their theme can be read as metaphor for a deeper quest to engage with the
hidden presence, the beautiful bride or the golden groom, who waits behind the veil of
ordinary appearance, willing to be won.
—FREYA MATHEWS

The real, therefore, is ultimately—and this again has been understood by all traditions—
not an object but a Person. A "Person" in this sense not by a human act of personification
of something in its innate reality neither living nor conscious; but rather human "persons"
are a manifestation in multitude of the single Person of Being itself, from which
consciousness and meaning are inseparable, these being innate qualities of life itself.
—KATHLEEN RAINE

Scarf

I heard you walking in the night
your bare foot in dirt
and the bells you wear about your ankle.
Quick jump and I was out, but already
your music was faint in the distance.
The night, however, was transfigured—
every bush held your fragrance
and the fields were strewn
with scarves you dropped.

Tomorrow by light
I will doubt you passed so near.
Perhaps some other night, you will wait.
You will loop a scarf about my neck
and holding its two ends
pull my face to yours.
I would be the white blossoms of Nicotiana
poised in the still air
for the soft panting moth-wings of you.

Bird

You are small as the bird
that barely sways the twig.

You lift on wings into blue air
and are gone.

Down in the roots
tree trembles
and earth in its darkness
turns again toward moon.

You are feather, toe
inciting eye
beak that breaks
the night in half
then weaves a nest
of wind and spilling hair.

By dawn it is proven
molten plumage
simmers as your eastern flank.

When at last you pass overhead
unaccountable updrafts
pull petals
from a full orchard of plums.

Night

You live in a tent by the sea
which is white
and bannered
and staked with the horns of narwhales.

When you burn small fires of driftwood
the walls light with slippery hues
of mother-of-pearl and your silhouetted shadow
moves about on indecipherable errands.

Outside the door is a garden
visible only through grief
when the world like caribou calf
has died frothy-mouthed on tundra.

You pick three flowers
float them in stone bath.
Near dawn step out
and a thin mist of resurrection

rises between your shoulders
and the fading scald of stars.

Door

You are the door earth opens
when it wants to walk into another season.

Because your threshold is strewn with leaves
the steps of life rustle with the holy.

In the meadow by the river
you are the arched lintel
bearing the rolling weight of sun
ever onward into its new heaven.

The more I am with you
the more the world leads only here
with sky a burrowing animal
pushing its nose into stars.

From your doorway, fragrance frees outward.
It lures like bower of twilight
where a gleam
skittering in on moth wing
can unfurl immeasurable
as banner of the moon.

Deer

You wash in morning river
      and again under rain of stars.
You are forever clean as rounded rocks
      as ridges molded to sky.
Why do you stand like a deer in the distance
      afraid to enter my camp?

Flower

Before the lifted flower fades look at me.

Tell me again the story of your birth.
And since we're crying
let's lay my death down
in the green blankets of this vale.

I would overturn every stone to find
the one continuity that carries to tomorrow.

Your skin is all the earth has ever made.
And under the sky where we walk weightless

everything seems so true
as to empty the air of space

and leave only the look of you.

Heron

Always I am feeling for you.
Small bird in leaves, my ear leaps.

Squirrel on limb and quick as a dancer
I'm on the verge where music breaks.

You are snow whose falling
lays bare rounded shapes of field.

On creek's bottom, a pebble waits
till the toe of stepping heron turns it over.

Then the seeing side is up, and I wonder
how you ever hid amidst this water and light.

Chickadees

Clouds have left no mark in the soft meadow of your skin
though they have passed there often these ages of quiet and stone.

Strong is flower scent in winds from up valley.
Time turns with half-smile in slow circles under sun.

Now it seems we only need dangle our arms
in water we did not make, the rest happens of itself.

Your toes in grass are pretty and cordial as chickadees.

Sway

Before that day by ocean
it seemed world was made of something
I could not know at crux
and all the talking of wind
as it moved through grasses and trees
was a conversation amongst others.

You wore a dress white as wings of gulls.
Ankle-deep you walked in reach of waves.
It was not merely that hours earlier
your sounds as they came forth close to ear
had broke open the encompassing night.

There was something else
I could not name then or now
neither foreground nor background
but everywhere like odor of sea.

You pointed to deer tracks in wet sand
but what you showed was also
starlight
brown beds of pine needles
narrow trails in forest dawn.

You walk just ahead of me now
a swaying shape I have always known.
When you lie down
I follow you into what we are.

Sheen

There is the forgotten curve of your waist
glimpsed from trail or from resting place
forgotten not as in lost
but remembered anew each time
barefoot step onto frost
all things crystalline and sudden
lips even in absolute dark.

It seems the curve of your waist
so easily erases distance
vaulting forward
as sound underwater
shouts of an everywhere
we can feel on our skin.

This world happens
like a caravan of travelers
strange and exotic in necklace and garb
moving on wheels we cannot understand

each moment shining
metal hammered to a sheen
that a thousand years ago
and a thousand years hence
is right now being fitted to your waist.

Invitation

You are tender as blue moth
dimpling petals of night.
Your skin is dusted with eternity—
how my hands ever glide
beyond what brings them back
to where they never left.

You are the seat earth takes
when it watches the young ankles of moon
just learning to walk.
You the bed sky reclines upon
when the weight of falling stars
tilts the sea toward sorrow.

I come before you like music
flooded with craving to be seen.
Look at me
bring me to life with your face
with the birds that live under your arms
and flare invitation when you lie back.

I am the excitement of a jewel
about to be placed on your neck.
Wear me. Wear me out.
May the sweat of love glisten.
May my singing body brave yours
to brim this world with anthem.

Closer

Seasons break over the bank with driftwood flailing.
The fallen tokens of our years
go the way of ancestors painted on rock walls.
All these days of my dying, something cried in my chest
as though it were three steps from heaven.

You were a young trout in pools of music and shade.
I prayed over our bed knowing tomorrow's dawns
were trails disappearing into mountains.

So often when you lie with me
it seems the hull of our boat leaks starlight
and our touch is candles floating past stones canopied in moss.

There was a day the willows arched over snow-melt water.
A day and another day and then a moon whose breath
was a silver mist we walked through.

Your voice comes to me now as it did then
pine needles falling onto snow.

If love buried its fragrance in this sagebrush
then it is your dance among them that wakens the worlds.

Appearance startles with what sanctions sight.
When you rise out of dark water, everything is there at once.
Tell me how it is we keep moving closer and closer.

Swallows

The river is in my dreams as you are
forever that is and everywhere at once
green pools and the dimpled skimmings of dragonflies.

I don't believe now there is anything but water
moving clear between boulders
big in the house built by us before we were born.

Home of sunlight and leaves
your hands hanging curtains deer will brush.

I don't believe now there is anything but you and I
river and dreams
moving from one end of time to the other
swallows fashioning nests below eaves of our roof.

Ten feet over the meadow their flights
pull threads of dimension out of thin air.
Nothing to build centuries upon but still it happens.
And from porch or hillock I could watch you forever
underneath the wings of swallows running.

She Said

Junco

A junco landed on her toe where she sat in sun
and the two looked at each other
with nonchalance of old friends.

Later between crumpled-granite uprisings
there was moonlight on sagebrush flats.
Clouds silent as deep water shapes
kept sliding frictionless over that unassailable light.

It was summer I remember
and warm for 10,000 feet.
The rest of the world waited over several ridges.

From under an isolated boulder
in the midst of green aspens
a tiny spring flowed.
When she touched her finger to that water
I heard no sound
but saw ripples in silver rings run outwards.

Bird Song

She said that if she cried
every morning
as she looked into light
I wasn't to worry; it was just
something like bird song
but salty and wet.

Moon

She said the moon once
slid through her hair
and she knew then what it was like
to be mouthed by the mother of things

a wet tongue cleaning all dust
and brittle accumulations
till she walked slick as a pebble—

and this in the desert
no river, no ocean—

she walked till the tongue in its wisdom
disappeared over mountains
and the morning star rising
in what was barely twilight

lit with a sheen
something she could only suppose
must be her own borderless skin.

Beauty Trail

Our last night she lit
fragrant sage and blessed me.
Sometimes wanderers meet
two leaves blown together in hollow log
and that rustling swirl
pulls horizon overhead
the suturing of a wound.

But the wanderer's world
is water-smoothed pebbles
thrown to wind.
Watch those stones turn to birds
and under the glinting wings
the wanderer follows.
That's the beauty trail, she said.

Blue mist of burning sage
drifted out among river willows.
She was wisp clouds turning red at sunset
then leaching further between the stars.

I can hear the ocean now
though I walk among inland mountains.
I will end up in the sea
that much I know
home of wanderers

join company with these granite mountains
and follow the lit and the shadowy wings
until they plummet into waves.

The beauty trail was easy
when her lips were here to sing it.

Strawberries

Once a woman who came to feel like a lake
when the first drops of rain are just reaching it
turned down a trail
and walked out of the light that she knew
into a different light. It seemed

more full of greens perhaps
certainly more full of space
and time she thought later
wrapped through like a snake
such that she could not tell
whether she was inside or out.

There were grasses
moving tops in some kind of wind
and even to the periphery
flashes of bird flight
yet it seemed like sky in its distance
had let fall something
that encased her and the land around her

such that she could not distinguish
what was time and what was light—
and so there was no movement really
she stood there or walked there or sang there
or all of them at once she did not know

for some duration
that was independent of beginning and end.

She felt for her face
which was wet on the cheeks
and she said that was the first piece to wash up
each a puzzle initially but one by one she held them
the taste of strawberries for instance or her husband's lips
a certain doorway, a wood pile
and weightless they fell into her
as though she had no bottom or top
just a depth that henceforth
all her days would neither fill nor empty.

Deer Beds

She said her secret was nothing but this:
deer sleep in small beds under trees.
You can get on all fours, find hairs
rubbed loose in among leaves and duff.
You can hold them in light
pale-brown and slender
your fingertips can feel them.
That's it, she said, and walked off
and I thought there must be more
not that deer don't sleep in beds under trees
but more to the secret
that she a week ago promised to tell
and I waited for, knowing that something
had happened, because she wasn't this way
three years ago, or even two, and it must
be about God or some insight so shattering
she cried into splinters, burned, fell as rain.
That's right she said
rain through leaves down into beds of deer.

Mermaid

Long after the hermit thrush
had ceased its seasonal singing
I was listening for it still
in trees beyond meadow's edge

as though it were a necklace
you had borne from sea
a song liquid luminescent
on throat of earth and air.

But that music was only present
with living moisture of your skin
and only when dwindling day had dampened
the tenor of light and wind.

Lupines are scenting the coast
wild irises melt into twilight.
Now I see the stars
turning in the mirror of your hand.

Maybe you heard the call of waves
and went out; maybe the necklace
is already a mile down. You always said
only a drowning man could love you.

Triumph

You were born in aspen grove that much I know
or dreamed there at least in green quiver of afternoon.

Perhaps I should worry more about my own death
then watching nighthawks take wing just past sunset.

Or the twilight deer descending to meadow
opening your night robe with grazing lips.

I found a place in high rocks I may never go to again
unless ghosts can cry for one more chance at old triumphs.

And on ridge of scrubby sagebrush, sign of puma
scoured smell of a thousand miles walked alone.

An old lament longs to root in stone of this mountain
conform to one fissure of that dark content.

But bath in cold stream only scatters the trout
and bestows no access to your barefoot stroll as stars fade.

One of these years for sure when aspens turn yellow
you're going to free my heart into the first frosty wind.

River

All night river moved with its easy swirls
and willows held still in star-bright cool.

She woke before me and walked to bank
her steps easy as nowhere to go.

      People worry whether love will last.

She brings me water, saying
"the river wanders through its home made of time".

Nothing is solid. Even the landscape
sifts beyond the muscles of my knowing.

Yet light can never drain altogether from sky
because there's no attempt to store it.

Less than arm's stretch away
she looks at me now from river's home.

      Her eyes have no worry.

Dogwood Bloom

If love came through forest
ducking head under branches as she walked
you would not say
"wait until the dogwoods bloom."

Early spring, that white flowering
will happen soon enough.
But love steps on moments that are already here.

Three deer move across meadow
leaving silver swaths in dewy grass.
(How can days this big keep appearing
as though out of imperceptible pocket?)

You lie at night, listening:
frogs, owls......something else.
She might arrive with morning light
how in treetops it wingless lands.

She's put a dogwood bloom in hair.
Even by starlight you can tell.
There's another in hand
like firefly or moon or night shine of ocean.

Now she's close enough
to trace petal tip from forehead
slowly down toward your chest.

You could die before it opens.

Reluctant Farewell at a Small Sierran Lake

My whole life I've been a walker in rains
carrying some small sorrow
like wren in cupped hands.

I've kept to gossamer trails of deer
coots calling from marsh
and light drops hitting lake with a thousand rings.

If this has been burden
it has bowed me down
like trees under sparkling dust of snow.

Look, you say, there are clouds in the lake
lakes in the clouds—
everything's in everything else.

      Oh, please, not now
      that tale of oneness
      praising ocean to discount the wave.

Water drips from your raven hair
making even mountains moan
when at last they must turn and go.

Once Upon a Time

A song of the rolling earth, and of words according,
Were you thinking that those were the words, those upright lines?
those curves, angles, dots?
No, those are not the words, the substantial words are in the ground and sea,
They are in the air, they are in you.
—WALT WHITMAN

Firstly, stories, like reality itself, deal in the particular,
not in abstraction and generality. If reality
is to communicate with us at all it will have to be via particulars,
since particulars are all it has—particulars
will necessarily form the elements of any "vocabulary" available
to it. Secondly, particulars in stories are strung together in patterns of significance,
patterns that resonate with what is most important to us as precarious beings
living in a beautiful but dangerous world.
—FREYA MATHEWS

Of course! the path to heaven
doesn't lie down in flat miles.
It's in the Imagination
with which you perceive
this world, and the gestures
with which you honor it.
—MARY OLIVER

Once

1.
Once the river felt it was not a river
but a deer, and ran as deer do over night earth.
I never supposed events like that could happen
not at least when I was at hand.
Maybe it was my feet in the water of your singing.
Maybe it was starlight on patch of snow
the silver of your beauty shining inward to itself.
Once the river ran on hooves
I could feel upon me like rain on a clear night
and everything that had lingered behind
came forward and fell into the running.
Rivers and nights, rain, legs whose length
stretch into a vanishing point.
Once the deer nosed through willows
and quietly across moonlit river waded.

2.
Once I believed in pastures of rain
and could walk there among shining stones
and leaning arms of grass. Once
I grazed on the green melody of earth
and the songs I knew fell from trees
like clear eyes that loved me.
I was a carpet of emerald moss
cushioning your feet as you walked.
I was a hollow of shade where the rabbit rested.

Once I could touch the root of spring
and bloom as easily as I can die.
I was the light and the air
and you were the sound of stars
that slept like seeds in the fruit of my hand.

3.
Once in its journey it seemed the sun
pulled all that I thought I was
and laid it out on a dresser top
like coins from a pocket—
everything now small, incidental
tapering down to a thinness
I could feel through.

The sky was a roof lifted away
the moment left alone as itself
irrefutable as sun
but also as unlookable
revealing but not in itself revealed.
I sat there by river
by green willows
as though opened to a flavor
that had always been on tip of tongue
not quite speakable
yet even my toes in their bluntness
were made of it.
The willows took me in their motion
and broomed it up and down the river
like dust the careless sun had dropped.

Rock, Fence Posts, Snow

1.

The rock is grey and large. Its top makes a curving arch as though a grey moon were rising up out of earth, rising without fissure or rumble, just a steady lifting silent as mushrooms in night, until the great disc clears ground, clears treetops, sails away into clouds, lost into clouds. Two months later a fisherman off coast of Mexico squinting into setting sun sees a grey shape enter the ocean, says it lowered itself down from sky like a spider, slid into sea without splash. He rowed boat home, lit a candle that night. In town square there was music and laughter, the skirts of the women swirling like moonlit water where an oar has dipped.

2.

Three old fence posts in the meadow. They hold their heads up like coyotes peering over brown grass. Fifty years, maybe more, of vigilance, a face at a window, waiting. The models of cars have changed, and many lie rusted in junkyards. Fog moves over the meadow like cows, sound of surf in their low-hanging bellies. A lantern swings in the night, and a long-haired woman goes to barn to make bed for the stranger. He came on foot from upcoast holding the ragged wing of a gull. Doors of barn creak, and chickens murmur from their roosts. The woman smells of hay, ringlets of her hair are beaded with fog while the strange man waits in the kitchen, hands folded neat as a cup on the plank table. He sits straight and perfectly still though the right side of his lower lip trembles slightly like a small pebble rolling to and fro under the waves.

3.

It is an early-autumn snow flurry in the Sierras, and flakes are falling into the fire. They are also falling into the lake and onto granite slabs, pine needles, clumps of grass. The flakes that fall into fire are like pebbles dropped into the deepest well. They come out in another country, whistling already the tunes of that land. A young boy leading goats hears the whistling and joins in with his pipes. The music carries across the meadow to a stream on the far side where sits a woman mute since childhood. She is etching poems onto wood chips and floating them like small rafts down the stream. She rarely looks up from her work. Mothers and children bring her cups of milk and bowls of grain. Wood cutters, bearded and sweaty, stop in their swinging to pick up and pocket the cleanest chips, and later they bring them to the woman by the stream, let them fall from their coarse hands silent as snowflakes. All the way down at the ocean, her work is washing up, which the people there gather for the colors released when thrown into fire.

Almost Home

We were almost home in sound of clear water
flowing over grey rocks through narrow cut
in wall of mountain rising above the sea.

Alder and willow lined beds of mint
asleep in shade under low arms of fir.

How in grassy flats, poppies
like days of light themselves
opened and closed in a brightness
we could not hold within our eyes
but surged pristinely through
to touch what exceeded us
like wind everywhere at once
the nearest shaken leaf
continuous with whitecap
edging farthest horizon.

It seemed even that beyond light and wind
and the impossible blue company of the sea
we were at home with something
we could not quite name as ourselves

pointing instead to a deer
stepping out onto light-washed slopes
as though that were an event
and not simply the way we are.

Three Men Pass

Three men pass by on horseback
and you think they can't be trusted.
That night the fire is jumpy.
When morning comes
we plunge into the river
and let it take us far from any place of fear.
Your arms are around my neck
when we wash up on a sand bar.
The three men are nearby.
They have caught a salmon
and we eat with them.
Later one plays guitar with back against tree.
The other two are chuckling
as they shuffle a deck of cards.
Off to ourselves
you are naked and sun-warmed as your toes
when I reach to kiss you.
The horses turn their heads for a second
then go back to cropping the tall grass.

Wild Iris, Lost Coast

In this thick wood of Douglas fir
a cloistered stillness hangs
and hidden therein, this wild iris.

Her bare-soled steps
make no sound on cool marble.
As she walks past empty pews to the altar
the long slender stem of her spine
exalts in her near weightless head
a violet-toned unfurling
dawn through stained glass.

A single penitent kneels at his vigil
his face streaked with anguish and self-contempt.
She has water in hand, and she sprinkles it.

Outside is a meadow
and the benediction of the iris
runs naked down that field to the sea
where it dives, with pelicans
headfirst into waves.

All along the coast
in the glory of blue and white
those fallen birds raise up their throats
and swallowed fish
become the lift of wings!

Frog By Granite Creek

It was small on the big rock
olive with coppery tinge.
Sun was hot. I sat
still wet from bathing.

It made no noise
when closer it hopped.

Entered a puddle I had dripped
and squatted a while therein.

Then emerged
to crawl under shady crevice
of my left foot.

Peered out a while
emerged again.

Looked up a while
paused a while
readied legs for a larger leap...

    and then did so

        landing to harbor in my pubic hair.
        I was happy to have it there.

Taste

Before sun has reached tree tops
you have gone for water
where beneath dark heave of rock
it issues like understudy of light.

But laying still where we have slept
I dream it is I going for water
and soft-soled in first dawn
it's over your forest body I walk.

Then I find myself on path
that has both bear track and deer.
Before me at base of dim boulder
you crouch absorbed over source.

When your hand raises water to lip
I taste dark earth-clasp of tree root
and know we are one body of sky
lifting beyond legend of leaf tip.

Desert Boat

A man is walking down a dry wash.
A raven flies by.
Its wings make the rough pulling sound of oars
boat rowed across lake of desert air.

On the far shore is a temple
where the passengers disembark
and walk among stone columns
and free-standing sculptures of beaked deities.

Wind blows from a fissure in ground
over which three strings are stretched.
They are tuned to the sound sky makes
when it thinks beyond beginning and end.

A lizard crawls from crack in temple
and cocks its head to one side.
It sees man walking in wash
and raven flying by.

Breaking Camp After
Ten Days Under Desert Cottonwoods

Once I was alone in the silence again.
The others had returned down trail
and I was to follow. But it seemed then

I was standing in what had preceded us
as though nothing whatsoever had happened.

Then it dawned that of course this was the afterlife.
All that took place could not be brought here.

Our days were pottery that crumbles in its firing.
I could not find the bowl of laughter
or the candle holder that held the light of eyes.

Remotely I could remember leaves of willow
etched in clay as though lines of grace
might last beyond their happening.

But I am standing now in the afterlife
from which the world like the desert
seems both elaborate and spare

and I am voiceless to sound down trail
that we have been here all along.

Sonoran Rhythms

Falling mountains
and light that fissures through the clouds.

How the mountains fall
full of bells and bountiful horses.

Two ravens roam the roomy sky
trailing rain
through coarse hair of sycamores.

Falling mountains
and feathered rakings of rain.
Feathered rakings of rain
and falling mountains.

How the rain is full of horses and bells.
How the beautiful light rings off rock.

Two ravens fall
through fissures in the clouds
and rising to meet them
the mountains and the rain.

Zen

I went out following the scent of grasses
and came back following the falling flowers.
—CH'ANG SHA

The light of our true nature is something that is autonomous and
natural, and it can't be stopped. It just bubbles up all the time and is
all around us. Everywhere you look, that's it! Everything you look
at, that's it!
—JOHN TARRANT

...the swallows grew still and bats came out light as breath
around the stranger by himself in the echoes
what did I have to do with anything I could remember
all I did not know went on beginning around me....
—W.S. MERWIN

Desert Rain

Waking at night to rain
light as pinch of salt

but one small cloud
most of sky
still showing stars

this is the way it must happen
love and death
all things both endless and terminal

just like this
barely more than dream

alone in desert shrubs
no substance
face of stars and rain.

Juniper Branch

The juniper branch holds raindrops
as though they were its own berries.

Yellow and orange the colors of autumn
cling to riverbanks, and like hair in water
this dreamy day floats through its own eddies.

Grey is granite valley, grey the sky.
And as always reasons to love surpass naming
numerous as kernels squirrels bury.

World mutes in rain—edges blur, colors run.
The buried kernels sprout, invisible in earth and air.
Their fine filaments cinch us deeper.

We're no longer sitting in a time and place—
we're made of what allows time and place.

The Mechanic

Early morning, and out of habit
I scan for some place
where I can mend my life
like a mechanic rolling from bed
on Sunday morning to slide
under his own car and tinker.

I bring the usual tools
and prod the usual places.
Nothing fits though this morning—
the sockets are wrong size
wrenches won't close.
What's worse, the darn thing
seems to be running fine.

The Way of the Shower

After sliding shut the shower door
I stand towel-wrapped.

Vapor swirls
in the upper reaches of the bathroom.

It's slow clouds
gliding up the glacier-carved valley of the Hoh.

Twisting, flowing
silently curling in and curling out

the great Tao plays right here
fogs down across the mirror
revealing it
clean of face.

After Singing

After singing, fall into quiet.
Lay down the rattle
like bones at end of journey.

Shadow has a taste
that sunlight longs for.

Sometimes we let go the foot of raven
and drop under a stone
that hasn't moved since the mountain rose.

    I can leave all this doing
    as though it were a handful of dust.
    A year's effort settles into nothing.
    One pass of the broom—gone.

    That's the clean house
    where Han-shan wore his dirty robes.

Desert Music

The door of music opens for a second
and a single note spills out.

It wanders long through desert
leaving narrow track for wind to fill.

When moon rises, the lonely one
lifts up arms to sing, while thirsty feet

drum earth for taste of water.
That dance becomes a cry the ocean hears.

Clouds arrive, and then there's no place outside
that room of stormy music, no door at all

just an inside being pelted by rain.

I Lean and Loaf in White Mountain Day

Young aspens
sprouting from runners
advance into sagebrush meadow.

They wobble like new-birthed fawns
blinking about for bearing.

Everywhere
wind
is blowing through nothing but naiveté
so fresh fear has yet to arise.

Openness is not an acquired trait.
It's prior to green leaves or wet tongue.

I've never left it in all my days of wandering.
No use reaching for it either.
It's like looking for Walt Whitman
but he's already told us
he's under our boot soles.

Wine

A man finished his dinner.
He left three bottles of wine on table.
Now the waiters and waitresses
are drinking them, laughing and carrying on.
It's a party at end of day.

Sometimes it's easy to see
that server and served bless each other.
Creek to ocean to rain to creek again
benevolence bows to benevolence.

Everyday, with a platter of dawn and dusk
the earth feeds us.
Be generous with the wine you leave.
Let a field of rain fall on the table.
By uncorking the luster interior to us
something pours into hollow places we cannot see
and the earth's party link arms
to tumble outward onto the streets.

Four Aces

Out in desert flats and along slopes
    meandering among rocks and shrubs
        the trail of wild horses

where they have walked and will walk
    the young, old, the new young
        who arise like flowers out of rain and dust

and pass then into bones that will lie
    spread out in gravel wash like a story
        the best story because it's the only story

the same one told over and over
    just color of fur changed or length of leg
        you remember it from that day

wind picked up cottonwood leaves
    blew them along ground we were going
        lest we forget

that between here and everywhere is no distance
    the trails and hooves and fading flowers
        go nowhere they aren't already

and the miner who a century or so ago
     lost the first horse to the wild
          is holding four aces and telling the story of nowhere

behind the tender eyes
     of every bar girl
          he meets in his travels.

Empty Round Bowl

The days are a rounding curvature
the inside of a bowl.
I could be anywhere, everywhere.
The wind flutters aspen leaves
and ages swirl like a roulette wheel.

I come to a time and place but loosely
dissolved in a broth of light
and the appearing shapes of earth.

One drink of what I am
and the bowl is the sky
clean of what never happens but always will.

On a Treeless High Mountain Ridge

The slicing flight of the swift
passing by
quicker
than the head can turn.

Wing rush
crescendoing—
then gone.

Now depth of air
not empty
but full
of sharp-veering
geometry

and now
mountain space
not other
than blue mind.

Under a Tree Looking Up

I am lying beneath tree.
It is a maple by the river
and the winds that have some bond with the river
are moving the leaves of that tree
while the sky beyond
is blue of late afternoon.

Nothing more is happening
so simple in the telling
but now it seems the blue beyond
is also where my head lays looking
and the moving of the leaves
is now held
within something unmoving
which is colorless really
though all color possible to it.

The local robin its nest nearby
alights on breezy twig
and looks at me
lucid eye
sees I suppose my harmless form

though it feels for the life of me
like the bird is within me
and so has to be looking
at nothing at all.

Remembering Chuang Tzu
in the California Desert

I dreamed I heard a mockingbird sing in the desert
and it sang of a place I had been long ago

but that long ago was in yet another dream
and so the dreaming-self was remembering another dreaming-self

everything is made of nothing really
all filmy and transparent

now I walk under desert cottonwoods
while the mockingbird sings from a mesquite

and small patches of snow
hang still in the higher mountains

at night I dream of the bird
visiting the spring hidden in thicket

drops glisten on its beak
when it raises its head to look at me.

Laundry

To be talked to under trees in slow morning—
you can feel that voice like fingers uncreasing all the folds.

You are laundry hanging
that someone else can come along and wear.

Someone you have never met, that no one has met
that comes along and goes out inside you

because it is morning under trees
and you are nothing except what always fills you.

You can wander that way, well-washed
and now drying, now spreading outward.

You may remember that yesterday was the same
the day before as well.

Even when you thought you were someone
and wore your clothing tight, you were not

not at least someone that anyone could meet
just garments clean as the morning under trees.

Leaf

In the meantime, I forget my own life
as though it were a leaf on water
fine in its own right, in fact qualified
and quite able to take care of itself
journeying down the water
no one even on the bridge to shout advice
toss flowers, wave it along

just the leaf let to go
bouncing off rocks as it will
undented
swirling through pools
undizzy

leaf afloat
water taking it wherever water goes.

A Day

Nothing was done that day in the mountains
and nothing was left undone.

Breezes shook grass stems
and as the sun moved
shadows eased eastward.

He sat by the lake and watched
the appearance of motion—
waves flowing
to their own emptiness at shore.

When night came he laughed:
How can I be said to be a day older?

Epilogue

The appropriate response to a world conceived as subject seems rather to be to seek to encounter it. To encounter another is to approach them as one with whom it is possible to have a relationship and from whom one can expect a response.
—FREYA MATHEWS

We are Nature, long have we been absent, but now we return,
We become plants, trunks, foliage, roots, bark,
we are bedded in the ground, we are rocks,
we are oaks, we grow in the openings side by side....
—WALT WHITMAN

For me you are a treasure more laden
with immensity than the sea and its branches
and you are white and blue and spacious like
the earth at vintage time.
In that territory,
from your feet to your brow,
walking, walking, walking,
I shall spend my life.
—PABLO NERUDA

I'm caught in this curling energy! Your hair!
Whoever's calm and sensible is insane!
—RUMI

Uncallused Hand

1.

You were forever telling me something I could not name
as though it hummed from grass where I lay in autumn
or from white and pink granite
rising into shapes above sagebrush and tree
from sky itself alone in its blue
or from line of mountain one behind the other unending
so on and so on dropping ever further into uncertainty
both what you were saying and how you could be saying it.
I watched as half moon rose in afternoon sky
and far-up sinuous glints of spider thread
came unrushed into airborne being
only to elapse as easy to a nowhere you are not.
    Let me lie in mountain pass circle of stone
    while some unruffled surface beyond wind
    slowly flecks white with dust of wild horse bone.

2.

So easily day dissolves to become part of a history
that fades like trail altogether into grass and woods.
No one will know we walked here
in all immediacy of light and location.
There was one who strung arrow at dawn
and brought back sheep from mountain slope.
His legs were strong and he used them in his loving.
All that's left of his way is flake of obsidian stone

where our new step bright and earnest crosses his.
Layer upon layer they weave together.
Something beautiful is being made.
Lightly now the sun has reached the aspen tips.
This strand falls in and away even as it happens.
Occasionally we feel the weight of the larger weave
invisible from any height because made of depth
occasionally the hunter lies down with his woman still
    and pulls over them blanket of rabbit fur
    while moon lays silver water upon sleeping land
    drowning them into what they always were.

3.
I barely knew I was listening to you
when I walked through streaming grass
though your hands rest at times in your lap
with the same nostalgia for love
as fields falling under folds of autumn light.
Nor was I thinking of you
when the doe eyes upright and patient as water
stepped slow between close columns of aspen trunks.
So often you are after-tone—a green canopy
cloistering movements both solemn and fragrant.
    Now I am turning toward sky's blue deluge
    now I am turning toward the earth you cry upon
    when twilight shoulders bow down toward refuge.

4.
And so the days pass
one hand sliding over a surface it loves

that point of touch so infinite and empty
smaller than leaf on back of turning earth
yet your body arches when I love it
and small birds hop the floor in shadowed forest light.
Over field after field the smell of sagebrush drifts
as though it had its own being.
Last night this morning now
everything seems to be happening
as though it were not dying
    as though it were only springing forth anew
    arching as it always does
    toward the uncallused hand of you.

About the Author

Walker Abel lives at a remote home in the Yolla Bolly Mountains of northern California. As an undergraduate at University of California, Santa Cruz, in the mid-70's, he participated in an environmental studies field program called Sierra Institute. Twelve years later, after completing a graduate program with ecopsychology pioneer Robert Greenway, he came back to teach for Sierra Institute, which he has done now for 26 years, while also taking on the role of director since 2003. Most of his poetry has been written in field journals while out on these academic programs, which are 9 weeks long and are entirely taught during a series of backpacking trips. It has not been unusual for Walker to teach three programs a year, amounting to a total of up to 6 months in the backcountry. One of his greatest joys is watching each new group of students open over time to the transformative influence of wilderness immersion. Walker has a 33 year old son (Stuart), who is also an ecopsychologist, backpacker, and nature-connection educator.

HOMEBOUND
PUBLICATIONS

At Homebound Publications we publish books written by soul-oriented individuals putting forth their works in an effort to restore depth, highlight truth, and improve the quality of living for their readers.

As an independent publisher we strive to ensure that "the mainstream is not the only stream." It is our intention to revive contemplative storytelling. Through our titles we aim to introduce new perspectives that will directly aid mankind in the trials we face at present as a global village.

At Homebound Publications we value authenticity and fresh ideas. From the submissions process where we choose our projects, through the editing phase, through the design and layout, and right to the crafting of each finished book, our focus is to produce a reading experience that will change the lives of our patrons.

So often in this age of commerce, entertainment supersedes growth; books of lesser integrity but higher marketability are chosen over those with much-needed truth but a smaller audience. We focus on the quality of the truth and insight present within a project before any other considerations.

Printed in the USA
CPSIA information can be obtained
at www.ICGtesting.com
JSHW082222140824
68134JS00015B/692